MODELS
OF
GROUP THERAPY

Second Edition

MODELS
OF
GROUP THERAPY

John B. P. Shaffer
Queens College of the City University of New York

M. David Galinsky
University of North Carolina at Chapel Hill

 PRENTICE HALL Englewood Cliffs, New Jersey 07632

Library of Congress Cataloging-in-Publication Data

Shaffer, John B. P., 1934-
    Models of group therapy / John B.P. Shaffer, M. David Galinsky. --
2nd ed.
        p. cm.
    Rev. ed. of: Models of group therapy and sensitivity training.
[1974]
    Bibliography: p.
    Includes indexes.
    ISBN 0-13-587916-7
    1. Group psychotherapy. 2. Group relations training.
I. Galinsky, M. David. II. Shaffer, John B. P., 1934-   Models of
group therapy and sensitivity training. III. Title.
    [DNLM: 1. Psychotherapy, Group.   WM 430 S525m]
RC488.S44 1989
616.89'152--dc19
DNLM/DLC
for Library of Congress   88-38423
                                                               CIP

Editorial/production supervision: Linda B. Pawelchak
Cover design: Wanda Lubelska
Manufacturing buyer: Ray Keating

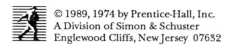
Printed in the United States of America

10 9 8 7 6 5 4 3 2 1

ISBN   0-13-587916-7

Prentice-Hall International (UK) Limited, *London*
Prentice-Hall of Australia Pty. Limited, *Sydney*
Prentice-Hall of Canada Inc., *Toronto*
Prentice-Hall Hispanoamericana, S.A., *Mexico*
Prentice-Hall of India Private Limited, *New Delhi*
Prentice-Hall of Japan, Inc., *Tokyo*
Simon & Schuster Asia Pte. Ltd., *Singapore*
Editora Prentice-Hall do Brasil, Ltda., *Rio de Janeiro*

To Judy, Derek, and Evan
and
To Dana, Michael, and Adam

CONTENTS

PREFACE

In preparing the second edition of Models of Group Therapy, it has been our conviction that the twelve group models of interaction surveyed here—whether formally falling within the field of psychotherapy, education, or social work—when taken together present a comprehensive overview of the current state of the field. Our work on this volume has been greatly assisted by feedback from reviewers, colleagues, students, and readers. As a result of such communications to us, as well as of changes in the field, many chapters have undergone extensive revision. Furthermore, one entirely new chapter —on self-help groups—owes its existence to our correspondents' insistence that the self-help group has emerged as a major model or format, and to our concurrence with this view.

What the models have in common is that each of them requires a finite number of participants (with fairly specific limits as to the minimum and maximum numbers); each offers a designated leader who has a clear-cut role in promoting the desired group interaction and some rationale as to what the primary content of the group interaction should be; and each attempts to provide the participant with a significant emotional experience that can prove instrumental in engendering new learning or change.

Our wish is to clearly conceptualize each model in its original form. We assume that the reader, having some interest in small-group practice, is curious about the *zeitgeist* within which a model developed and about the people involved in its creation. We also have some practical aims in mind—particularly the necessity that a group leader have a clear view of the conceptual model that he or she is employing and of the purposes for which that particular group is to be used. And there are many reasons why a skilled leader should be conversant with several group models. For example, one would hope that group leaders who conduct one-day community sessions to discuss the problem of drug abuse would employ a different approach from that which they use in conducting their weekly, considerably smaller, psychotherapy groups.

This kind of conceptual clarity seems especially important in the case of the novice leader. One often hears statements to the effect that the well-trained group leader (let's call him John Jones) does "his particular thing" no matter what the formal label of the group he is leading may be and that his group participants are being given an experience in, and demonstration of, John Jones as much as they are a demonstration of what a "T-", "encounter," or "gestalt-therapy" group is like. This might well be true, because John Jones, as a skilled leader, has probably, over time, developed a coherent framework with idiosyncratic features (just as it is often true of the trained psychotherapist, who may similarly arrive at an individual form of disciplined eclecticism). But where would this therapist or group leader have been at the beginning of this training without systematic models to study, internalize, and assimilate? While reality and models of reality are not the same thing, a model can provide an important guide to concrete practice, and it is our belief that external models (however much they may be subsequently revised, reordered, and partially discarded as a consequence of experience and evaluation) are still important to the socialization process of the professional leader or therapist. A thorough understanding of one or more clearly conceptualized models of group interaction is still probably the best basis from which to begin to search for one's own unique style of group leading.

Moreover, since each model represents a specific attempt to meet a specific goal, the intelligently eclectic group leader may wish to incorporate features of more than one model in leading his various groups (and for this, a detailed knowledge of all the primary models is needed). For instance, while the encounter group model offers some ingenious techniques for helping people to contact their feelings and fantasies, the T-group constitutes a powerful tool for emphasizing group cohesion and group dynamics (since its single task is to observe, and conceptualize, the group interaction as it is occurring). The encounter leader familiar with only the encounter model might well tend to neglect powerful forces for cohesion and for group autonomy existent within the group, whereas a familiarity with the T-group enables him to more easily mobilize group-cohesive forces (e.g., by intentionally making fewer interventions early in the group, by allowing members to take therapeutic responsibility for each other, and by encouraging the group to examine norms, like suppression of anger, that tend to work against cohesion).

A problem that was bound to confront us was the decision as to which models to include. Our eventual breakdown of existing group methods into twelve distinct models in itself constitutes a model of sorts: *our* conception of how the diverse strands of current group practice can best be ordered and classified. All models are in a sense arbitrary in their emphasizing certain data-clusters and neglecting others; we have no doubt that different authors would have produced a somewhat different organization of group models.

Four of our group therapy models represent an extension of what was initially a model of individual psychotherapy to a group context; these are the psychoanalytic, existential-experiential, gestalt therapy, and behavior modification groups. We include them because of this historical and theoretical importance, their widespread use, and their influence on the development of later group models. However, were we to have included all group models emanating from a theory of personality or of individual treatment, we would have to had to present such a bewildering array of models that the book would have lost much of its instructional value. Therefore, models based on Adler's interpersonal therapy and Berne's transactional analysis, and so on, were rejected. Family therapy was excluded because it seemed too specific an application of psychotherapy and at the same time too broad and complex an area to treat in a single chapter; instead, it would seem to warrant a separate book in its own right.

When it came to the format for each chapter, we chose a flexible course wherein our schematic organization was geared to the particular model presented. All chapters contain a "Key Concepts" section and another section called "Role of the Leader." Where it seems appropriate, we present theoretical concepts and methodological concepts separately. Some of the chapters include an illustration of a typical group session. Others do not, especially if the model's theoretical presentation already has embedded within it examples of the kinds of group interaction that it encourages, or if the model is so complex that it comprises several submodels and is therefore too complicated for an extended illustration to really clarify or instruct.

Finally, we have endeavored to present each model in as impartial and nonevaluative fashion as possible. Our aim is for you, the reader, to understand the rationale of a model from the point of view of its creators and to appreciate what they perceive its unique assets and applications to be. It will then be left to you to decide, perhaps aided by your own classroom learning and/or teaching, and your own practice as a group leader, to decide which model or models are most valuable to you for you specific uses and needs.

MODELS
OF
GROUP THERAPY

CHAPTER ONE
HISTORICAL
INTRODUCTION
AND OVERVIEW

In the first edition of this book we thought it important to make a distinction between group psychotherapy models originating within a clinical context (the group leader is a psychotherapist, members seek help for a variety of symptoms or problems, and the group meets for an indefinite and extended time) and group models originating within a vocational or educational setting (the leader tends to be viewed as a trainer or facilitator and the participant as a relatively healthy person, the group interaction focuses on a specific issue or theme, and the group meets for a predetermined and limited period of time). We referred to the latter as growth and development—or sensitivity-training—groups, and our original title, *Models of Group Therapy and Sensitivity Training,* reflected the distinction between these two kinds of groups.

Today this distinction has become tenuous, for more and more professionally led psychotherapy groups are (1) situation-specific in their focus, (2) designed for participants who need not present any serious psychological symptomatology, but who have a common issue or problem to contend with, and (3) either open-ended (patients may join or drop out at any point) or time-limited in their duration (e.g., a group for chronically ill patients and their families). Consequently it appears to us that all modern group methods are inherently therapeutic in their aims, and it is this view that is reflected in our current title, *Models of Group Therapy.*

EARLY BEGINNINGS

The first model that we present is the social work group. While such groups have a more community-based and reality-oriented purpose than the typical therapy group, the earliest social work group, by bringing together people having common social, economic, and personal problems, was a historic forerunner of modern group psychotherapy. Its earliest and most dramatic milestone was the opening of Jane Addams's Hull House in 1889. On the basis of the model set by Hull House, the early phase of group work developed primarily as a means of providing help for the increasingly large number of people served by settlement houses in the late nineteenth and early twentieth centuries. With social reform as a guiding ideal, groups were organized to agitate for better housing, recreation, and working conditions. Later other kinds of social agencies, including such religiously supported private organizations as Catholic Charities and Jewish Family Service, became integrally involved with the development of social work groups. Slowly the field began to include groups concerned with the immediate personal needs of its members, as well as with the amelioration of adverse social conditions in their communities, thus moving closer to the person-focused orientation that characterizes most psychotherapy groups. However, social group work has never abandoned its fundamental interest in the larger social community in which group members have common origins, origins that in turn provide them with a basis for shared needs and goals. In this respect, the group work model bears some likeness to later therapy groups emphasizing the participants' membership in a common social system or organization (e.g., the Tavistock, T-group, and theme-centered models).

As if to bear out the fine line existing between social group work and group psychotherapy, the group traditionally credited with being the first therapy group proper was one in which members shared both a common problem or symptom—advanced tuberculosis—and a similar, somewhat impoverished, environment. However, although bearing some resemblance to the social work group, this assemblage of tubercular patients, created as it was under the aegis of medicine and conducted by a physician, formally fell under the heading of "treatment." It began in 1905, when Joseph Hersey Pratt, a Boston internist, developed the "home sanatorium treatment" of consumption at Massachusetts General Hospital's Outpatient Clinic; virtually all histories of group therapy now credit Pratt with being the first practitioner of modern group therapy (Yalom, 1985). Designed for poor patients who were unable to afford inpatient treatment, Pratt's program organized outpatients into groups, or "classes," of roughly twenty people. Realizing that these disheartened people needed encouragement and supervision, Pratt directed his initial efforts at the kind of psychological approach that is often described as inspirational, persuasive, and supportive. He checked on the patients' progress and made precise prescriptions regarding such matters as diet, rest, and sleep. He was at pains to show group members that even in a slum environment they could approximate some of the elements of outdoor living emphasized in the sanatorium treatment of tuberculosis.

As time went on, Pratt became more sophisticated about the psychological aspects of the group's interaction. He appreciated the importance of an atmosphere of mutual support created by patients' having a "common bond in a common disease" (Spotnitz, 1961, p. 29), and he stressed the beneficial influence that one patient, especially if he or she were improving in health, could have upon another. Then, in 1918, when another physician, a psychiatrist named Edward W. Lazell, used a lecture approach to war veterans diagnosed as schizophrenic, medical group therapy was extended to patients suffering psychological disorders. Soon these patients' overall life adjustment, rather than their specific psychiatric symptom, was to be defined as a legitimate focus of the group's attention.

Until this point, practical procedures for starting and leading groups had taken precedence over formal theory, with the result that the theoretical rationale for what transpired in groups tended to be subsumed under a common-sense framework emphasizing the usefulness of instruction, advice, support, and a mutual identification among members. Under the impetus of such figures as Trigant Burrows (1927), Louis Wender (1936), and Paul Schilder (1936), the therapy group was gradually viewed within the conceptual framework of psychoanalysis, which had already had great influence as a theory of individual personality and a method of individual treatment. Burrows referred to his procedures as "group analysis"; Wender observed that transference phenomena developed within groups just as in individual psychoanalysis; and Schilder, in an attempt to incorporate into group therapy the Freudian technique of free association, encouraged a group patient to spontaneously discuss whatever came to his or her mind.

The consolidation of the psychoanalytic group model was left to the work of Samuel Slavson, Alexander Wolf, and Emanuel Schwartz. Slavson's initial experiments with groups had begun in his work with children and adolescents at the Jewish Board of Guardians during the 1930s. His orientation was a product of his personal experience as a psychoanalytic patient and his earlier employment in progressive education and recreational group work. He eventually came to call his approach *activity group therapy,* since it emphasized the importance of the expression of a child's conflicts and pent-up feelings through sports, games, arts and crafts, and other recreational activities. Subsequent outgrowths of activity group therapy involved play group therapy for preschool children, "activity-interview" therapy for older children, and finally "interview group therapy," which—since it emphasized communication via words rather than action or play—was essentially a form of analytic group therapy (Slavson, 1950).

Alexander Wolf, a psychiatrist and psychoanalyst, had become interested in group therapy during the early 1930s. Although no formal training in groups was available at that time, he read whatever was available, mainly the work of those already mentioned—Burrow, Schilder, and Wender. In 1938 he decided to experiment; he approached five men and five women who were patients of his and suggested that they enter a psychotherapy group. Within a year he was running four such groups. By 1947 Wolf had started to hold seminars in psychoanalytic group therapy at the New York Medical College. World War II had played an important role in stimulating an awareness of group therapy among younger psychotherapists in the armed services, since it enabled them to treat more patients than they would have been able to treat on an individual basis. After the war many of these men were themselves becoming patients in therapy groups in order to intensify their training. In 1948 Wolf began a similar training workshop at the Postgraduate Center for Mental Health in New York City, then called the Postgraduate Center for Psychotherapy. One of his early students was Emanuel Schwartz, who was also to join the staff of the Postgraduate Center and who co-authored with Wolf two books on what they prefer to call "psychoanalysis in groups" (Wolf & Schwartz, 1962; Wolf et al., 1970). By 1954 the Postgraduate Center had introduced a certification program in group therapy; psychoanalytic group therapy, now regarded as a specialization requiring formal training, had come of age.

More than any other writers in the field, Slavson, Wolf, and Schwartz stood for a systematic application of psychoanalytic concepts, particularly resistance, transference, and interpretation, to the group context. Although acknowledging that the presence of other patients added an extremely important variable to the treatment process, these analysts insisted that the ever more diverse and complex data of the group setting could still be subsumed and accounted for by orthodox analytic concepts or principles. The therapeutic task remained that of interpreting to the patient how his or her current attitudes toward the therapist and other people reflected both a defensive resistance to awareness and insight and an inappropriate carrying-over from the past, or transference, of earlier, often fearful, ways of relating to his or her parents. Now that there were other people present in therapy, these interpersonal attitudes could be more dramatically evidenced in a number of different interactions. As in individual psychoanalytic treatment, the most penetrating and effective interpretations were believed to be those that connected an ongoing emotional reaction in the treatment situation itself to a remembered, emotionally significant interaction pattern with important figures of the past. The closest the group psychoanalysts came to a revision of their concepts was in the introduction of the term *multiple transference,* which was designed to take into account the fact that in the group setting a patient's transference now manifested itself not only in relation to the analyst but to the other group members as well. In other words, these analysts were claiming that in psychoanalytic group therapy the single most important unit of conceptual analysis was to remain that of the individual personality, even though this personality was now being treated in a multi-person, as opposed to two-person, setting. Their remarks were specifically directed against advocates of a group-dynamics approach to psychotherapy, namely Foulkes (1965), Bion (1959), and Ezriel (1973) in Great Britain, who emphasized the importance of viewing the group as a coherent entity with its own inherent laws. The psychoanalytic approach insisted that the latters' concentration on group phenomena, while perhaps appropriate for training groups designed for the teaching of group dynamics, constituted an inappropriate conceptual emphasis in the case of therapy groups, where the individual patient and his or her psychodynamics must always remain the primary focus of conceptualization.

Needless to say, Foulkes, Bion, and Ezriel disagreed, along with two American group therapists, Whitaker and Lieberman (1965), who developed their own model of a group-dynamics approach to group psychotherapy. Interestingly enough, these theorists viewed themselves as never really departing from a psychoanalytic orientation, since they had been trained within it, subscribed to many of its conceptions of personality structure and personality development, and viewed psychological symptoms as a compromise between the expression of an impulse and the defense against it. Nevertheless they insisted that group psychotherapy must develop theoretical concepts that were germane to groups in their own right and not borrowed from the psychology of individuals, and they suggested that an appreciation of social psychology, wherein the group as a whole is regarded as a discrete entity, be added to the group therapist's background in clinical psychology or psychiatry.

The concept of the group as a genuine, organized, and dynamic organism in its own right, comparable to the integrity of the individual personality, was and probably still is hard for many people to accept, and for some may even have had, however subtle, fascistic and totalitarian connotations (Denes-Radomisli, 1971). The difficulty they have with it is in part due to psychological and ideological conceptions of the person that place high value on his or her individualism and personal autonomy and in part due to the fact that the single personality, as a function and property of a biologically distinct human being, is more easily envisaged as a separate force in its own right than is the more physically diffuse group. Yet the concept of an organized and coherent *personality*, like that of the *group-as-a-whole*, is still a hypothetical construct, and like other constructs (e.g., the *ego* or the *self*) need not have an essential correspondence to physical reality. Hence, just as one's personality could be seen by some theorists as a constellation of "introjects" or "selves," the group could be similarly viewed as an entity comprising a constellation of individual selves or persons. The behavior of any one person in the group cannot then be viewed as independent from the behavior of any other person or from the overall group interaction. Such a view has gained wider credence in clinical psychology and psychiatry in recent years, as concepts derived from *general systems theory* have become more familiar to clinicians (Durkin, 1981). The single clinical area that has received the most direct application of systems concepts has been family therapy, where the family is seen within the framework of a transactional communication network in which the child's behavior is in part a function of his or her parents' marital interaction and their interaction is in part a function of the child's behavior, and so on.

General systems theory, however, was hardly beginning to be developed at the time that Foulkes and Bion were applying their experience with British Army therapy groups to civilian therapy groups in the immediate post–World War II era. Instead, these men found Kurt Lewin's field theory (Lewin, 1952; Morrow, 1969), which may be viewed as an earlier prototype of general systems theory in that it too emphasized the need to see the group as a patterned whole, to be the most suitable conceptual framework for their purpose; they proceeded to combine psychoanalytic and field theory principles into the various combinations that constitute the three group-dynamic therapy models to be presented in Chapter 4. The practical effect of this theoretical focus was that the group therapist now carefully attended to the group interaction with an eye not so much toward what it revealed about the pathology or characteristic behaviors of each individual patient, but to the overall theme or group tension that it revealed to be common to all the patients. This *group process,* carefully nurtured and guided by the therapist, was seen to be the significant curative factor in treatment, rather than insightful interpretations directed toward a single patient's psychodynamics; hence the therapist's task was to attend to group process variables as much as to the content of individual members' concerns. Only by doing the former successfully could he or she make interventions that would keep group tensions and group avoidances in a state of optimum balance wherein members would feel encouraged to express themselves, but not at the cost of overwhelming anxiety or threat.

The next major group therapy model that was a clear departure from the psychoanalytic group was the existential-experiential model. It was largely an outgrowth of an existential approach to psychiatry and psychopathology that had originated in Europe, particularly in the work of Ludwig Binswanger and Medard Boss, and that subsequently became better known in the United States through the publication of *Existence,* edited by May, Angel, and Ellenberger (1958). This model's development was also stimulated by the contributions of certain American psychotherapists, among them Rogers (1967) and Whitaker and Malone (1953), who had already been experimenting with a more experiential approach to psychotherapy wherein therapists permitted themselves a greater openness and a more emotionally intense way of relating to their patients.

Like the group-dynamic therapy model, the existential-experiential model is psychoanalytic in its basic conceptual roots because of its fundamental grounding in the concept of unconscious motivation. What was new in its approach was a strongly humanistic dimension that emphasized ontological concepts involving the patient's "being" and the fundamental irreducibility of her psychological experience. While acknowledging that there were unconscious ramifications in what a patient verbalized, the existential analyst rejected a simplistic reductionism wherein a person's conscious experience was viewed as a mere surface "screen" for invisible, unfathomable forces. According to these analysts, a readiness to "interpret" and "analyze" a patient's inner life tended to make the therapist a greater expert on what the patient was "really" experiencing than she herself was, thereby reducing the patient to an object. Instead, any investigation of the unconscious had to have as its starting point a deep, abiding interest in and respect for the patient's view of herself and her world; this was always the primary datum and in this sense the existential-experiential approach was strongly phenomenological.

The experientialism of this approach had a reciprocal aspect in that the therapist's feeling reactions to the patient were to be as open and shared a part of the therapeutic transaction as was the patient's experience of the therapist. The experientialists, while not denying elements of transference and fantasy within the therapist-patient relationship, also wanted to acknowledge the profoundly real aspects of this relationship; their emphasis was on the mutuality of an authentic "I-thou" encounter between two living, experiencing—and therefore inherently equal—human beings. Hence for them the "blank screen" emphasis of the Freudians, wherein the therapist attempted to deemphasize his reality as a person, was a myth that could not succeed in hiding the fact that everything he did (or neglected to do), including his non-verbal behavior, revealed his fundamental being to the patient; it was this essential quality of his "being"—the person who the therapist was in the most fundamental sense—that was the crucial ingredient in therapy, rather than the specific characteristics of his technique. Such a conception helped the therapist to feel freer to relate in spontaneous and intuitive ways, to share with the patient his fantasies about her, and to perhaps even admit his irritation with some of the patient's resistances. A greater give-and-take between patient and therapist in individual therapy naturally extended to group treatment, where the therapist could now from time to time assume the role of another patient in the group, in the sense of acknowledging some of his own personal concerns, and all members could become more fluid in their expression of their feelings, in their ability to move from fantasy to reality and back again, and in their opportunity to now react to the feelings and fantasies about themselves revealed by the therapist.

As had been the case with the psychoanalytic model, the existential-experiential model moved from its origins in individual therapy to an application to groups without its proponents feeling the need for any fundamental theoretical reorientation. They did not see any particular usefulness in a specifically group-dynamics focus in their groups, and in fact did not address themselves to this issue. In general, the overt methodology of experiential groups did not differ markedly from that of the psychoanalytic group; unlike the psychodrama and gestalt therapy models, which we are about to discuss, communication was primarily conversational and unstructured, the analyst was nondirective, and patients continued to feel free to narrate in a conventional fashion "there-and-then" problems from their outside living. The difference in outlook between an analytic and an experiential approach related more to fairly subtle aspects of the therapist's basic attitude toward the patient and toward the therapeutic task. This shift, however, was eventually to lead to more and more behavioral freedom on the part of both therapist and patient and thereby to become one of the several factors influencing the subsequent development of the encounter model.

The next model to be considered is psychodrama. In a strict historical sense it is the oldest model extant, since it had been given some systematic formulation by its founder, Jacob Moreno, as early as 1910. As a premedical student, he spent time walking in the gardens of Vienna where he observed the seemingly therapeutic effect on children of their own spontaneous fantasy play, which often involved symbolic reenactment of difficult family situations. Indeed, psychodrama had taken on the properties of a formal model or system by 1921, when Moreno opened his Theatre of Spontaneity in Vienna, and it was Moreno who in 1932 first coined the term *group psychotherapy*. However, the influence of psychodrama on the development of group therapy as a whole has been diffuse and certainly less pronounced than that of the psychoanalytic and experiential models. The method's greatest impact has been on the creation of a specific technique, usually referred to as "role-playing," that is frequently employed by group leaders in conjunction with a variety of other procedures; this technique is employed most often by leaders of growth and development groups, but it is also used by eclectic group therapists, social group workers, behaviorally oriented group leaders, and innovative classroom teachers. Because this influence is usually not acknowledged, Moreno's feeling that his contributions have been slighted and underestimated by most official histories of group methods seems quite justified. Somewhat less prominent on the contemporary scene is the pure psychodrama group, in which role-enactment techniques are used exclusively. Most of the therapists who practice in this manner have been trained either directly by Moreno or at the Moreno Institute in New York. Even here it is our impression that many of these therapists are beginning to combine psychodrama techniques with some of the methods introduced by other group models, particularly gestalt and encounter.

Probably the most significant emphases introduced by Moreno involved those of action, empathic identification, and catharsis. While almost all approaches of group psychotherapy from Pratt onward had assumed that opportunities for mutual support and identification among members were therapeutically useful, it remained to Moreno's theoretical framework to take into the most systematic account the specific relationship between the patient whose problems were being highlighted at any particular time (the "protagonist") and the rest of the group (the "audience"). The processes whereby audience members, through empathic identification with the protagonist, gain help from him and, through their assumption of "auxiliary ego" roles, also give help to him, received careful attention in this model. Such a conceptualization was bound to bear on the processes involved in most therapy and training groups, for although psychodrama made the protagonist's role more formal, almost all models of group interaction, from psychoanalytic through encounter, involve a scenario in which one particular member, for however brief a period, assumes "stage center" while the remainder of the group focuses on that member.

Moreno's basic concern was to help a patient translate his specific psychological problems into a here-and-now, dramatic recapitulation of an important aspect of his life situation, so that both he and others could experience it in concrete, vivid, and visual terms, much as a sleeper's concerns are translated into dramatic, tangible form via his dreams. Moreno chose the method of dramatic action, whereas both the analytic and experiential models encouraged patients to talk *about* their problem in discursive, narrative, "there-and-then" ways, just as one might recount the plot of a play rather than enact it. Moreno's action technique was to have a very important influence on how Perls, in his founding of gestalt technology, and Schutz, in his formulation of encounter technique, were eventually to attempt to help group participants communicate their deepest feelings and conflicts. Central to this entire action method was the notion of catharsis—the belief that the protagonist, through a more masterful and effective living-through of past events in a dramatic form, could achieve the therapeutic release of hitherto unexpressed feelings. According to Moreno, Freud and Breuer—the two earliest psychoanalysts—had too quickly abandoned the hypnotic method through which several of their patients had succeeded in achieving crucially therapeutic catharses.

As we suggested above, a strong methodological connection exists between Moreno's psychodrama and Perls's gestalt therapy, one that is greater than Perls seemed willing to admit. Indeed, the gestalt format might be described as an essentially psychodramatic technique in which the same participant enacts all the major "roles" in her life, although in order to have an apt analogy we need to redefine roles in such a way that they include not only the patient herself and the other significant people in her life, but also aspects of herself, such as particular feelings, body parts, and introjects. However, while both Moreno and Perls consciously introduced a highly theatrical metaphor into their therapies, it should be pointed out that there are some fundamental philosophical differences between their respective approaches.

Perls's approach differed from Moreno's not only in its conceptual heritage (which was more rooted in formal psychological theory than was psychodrama), but also in its essential aim, for gestalt was consistently and solely directed toward effecting changes in the patient's awareness and not in encouraging specific means by which she could approach life situations differently. It is true that psychodrama also attempted to concern itself with intrapsychic change, especially in its emphasis on catharsis; yet its encouragement of rehearsals, particularly of pressing present and future events, bordered on an attempt to help the patient "solve" some of his interpersonal problems via different or more adaptive behavior and actually foreshadowed the behavioral group therapy model (Chapter 8), which was to place even more emphasis on the "practicing" of specific behaviors. This kind of concrete prescription for change—or what Perls called a "program"—was something that he eschewed. Instead the focus in gestalt therapy was always to be on what *is*, the moment-to-moment flow of awareness, and not on the "should bes" or "might have beens" of a patient's life.

The therapist's task was to help the patient get in better contact with her awareness continuum, through a variety of techniques that typically involved an exaggeration of certain mannerisms and behaviors, including nonverbal ones; his skill lay in his ability to circumvent the patient's typical employment of various behaviors, including interpersonal "games," as a way of avoiding emotionally painful areas. One means by which he facilitated the patient's awareness task was to minimize the amount of stimulation or group pressure impinging on the latter's phenomenological experience. In order to accomplish this the group was discouraged from interacting with the patient while she and the therapist were working together. In this respect, Perls went further than did any other theorist in isolating the patient "protagonist" from the "audience." Despite the fact that the overt action of the group was now confined to a therapist-patient dialogue similar to that of individual therapy, Perls found the group format to be highly advantageous, first because the presence of other people gave the therapist an opportunity to explore some of the patient's typical interpersonal distortions and fantasy "projections" in a direct and immediate way, and second because the other group members, as a kind of empathic "Greek chorus," could learn from, and resonate with, the patient's highly emotional experience (Denes-Radomisli, 1971). It was only a matter of time before other group models (e.g., Schutz's open encounter), where spontaneous member-to-member communications became a normal part of the group's interaction incorporated gestalt-therapy techniques into their methodology (albeit in a less rigid fashion) and before other gestalt therapists began to permit, and even encourage, spontaneous member-to-member interactions in the groups that they led (Polster & Polster, 1973; Feder & Ronall, 1980).

In turning our attention to the next group therapy model that we present—the behavioral approach—we introduce a school of psychology that, like psychoanalysis, has had an enormous influence on the social sciences in general, particularly as they have developed in the United States. Founded by an American psychologist, John Watson, during the 1920s and building on Pavlov's historic discovery of conditioning phenomena in both animals and humans, behaviorism saw one's entire personality as a complex constellation of specific stimulus-response connections that had been sequentially learned over the long period of individual development. Because of its fundamental foundation in animal learning, which could be studied under precise and controlled laboratory conditions, behaviorism developed as a part of experimental psychology, with the result that its initial thrust was in the area of basic research. However, its emphasis on the individual responding stably and differentially to the various stimulus properties of his environment was bound to have important applications to both education and psychotherapy. If a troubled individual could be reconditioned through a reordering of the stimuli to which he was exposed, new, more adaptive, "response hierarchies" could be established. Consequently, the emergence of *behavior modification* as an alternative approach to psychotherapy was one of the most significant developments within the field of clinical psychology during the late fifties and early sixties.

Although behavior modification, like most approaches to psychotherapy, initially had individual therapy as its main area of application, it was inevitable that it gradually become extended to a group context. Groups were seen as especially appropriate in handling more complex social behaviors involving shyness, assertiveness, and excessive anxiety around anger. In encouraging the patient to try out new behavior in repetitive and unsatisfying life situations, a behavioral approach has an obvious likeness to psychodrama, as we indicated previously. In both psychodrama and the behavioral practice group, role-playing has a prominent part, and a naive observer watching selected segments from both group approaches might well find them indistinguishable. Indeed, some practitioners of behavioral practice groups have acknowledged an indebtedness to the earlier model. In actuality, though, there are distinct differences between these two approaches, and these contrasts are not surprising in view of the fact that philosophically these models have quite divergent views of the individual. For example, psychodrama emphasizes spontaneity, free expression, and a loosely organized format, whereas structured and clearly articulated goals for specific behavior change are central to the behaviorally oriented group. Moreover, psychodrama, although concerned with behavior in specific life situations, also aims for intrapsychic changes, particularly those that result from catharsis, with the hope that these inner changes will subsequently and spontaneously, via unconscious processes, lead to different, not-to-be-prescribed behavior in the future, whereas the behavioral group therapist, through the practice of prescribed behavior, attempts to add concrete new responses to the patient's behavior repertoire.

LATER DEVELOPMENTS

The next four models to be considered—Tavistock, T-, encounter, and theme-centered—were not designed for people in personal distress, but for those who wished to enhance various aspects of their day-to-day lives; for this reason, these models are still sometimes described as "sensitivity-training" or "growth and development" groups. Psychodrama and gestalt, though at the outset primarily designed as clinical methods for troubled people, form a useful bridge to a consideration of the four models, for they sometimes introduced nonpatients, frequently psychotherapists themselves, into their membership as a means of demonstrating the therapeutic value of their method. Eventually some gestalt and psychodrama groups were to take the form of relatively brief training institutes, lasting anywhere from a day to a week.

The two earliest growth and development models were the Tavistock "small study" group and the T-group. Although differing in both national and theoretical heritage (Tavistock having originated in Great Britain within a psychoanalytic framework, and the T-group in the United States within the wide scope of behavioral-science theory), they had much in common: Both owed something to the seminal work of Kurt Lewin; both were directed toward enabling people to become more knowledgeable about group dynamics; both assigned the group the primary task of studying its own behavior; both attempted to keep the group as unstructured as possible (believing that the elimination of the hierarchies, fixed agendas, and quasi-parliamentary procedures encountered in traditional working groups would force to the surface those latent group issues and tensions that such routinization normally supressed); and both embedded their small-group experience as a basic foundation—or core learning experience—within a larger institute structure (called a "conference" by Tavistock and a "laboratory" by T-) in which other formal groupings also took place, including didactic sessions and larger group events.

The Tavistock small study group was an outgrowth of the group-dynamic psychotherapy model that we have already reviewed and was founded by Wilfred Bion, whom we have already mentioned in connection with the earlier model. Essentially a theorist, Bion found himself more and more interested in the ways in which *all groups,* whether large or small, therapy or nontherapy, go about their tasks, whatever their nature. The theory that he eventually arrived at viewed all groups as having a delicate balance between progressive and regressive forces, and he went on to establish universal laws of group development and group behavior that accounted for and explained these forces (Bion, 1959; Pines, 1985).

Unlike many other groups, the Tavistock small study group's only function was to scrutinize the data of its own behavior in order to formulate the principles underlying them. True to its psychoanalytic tradition, this model made a "patient" out of the group (since the psychoanalytic patient is similarly encouraged to examine his immediate feelings and thoughts in order to better understand his transference reactions). Furthering the group's being treated as a single person or entity was the leader's effort to consistently pitch his interpretations to the group-as-a-whole, rather than to any of its individual members.

The T-group was also concerned with group processes and with encouraging a group to become aware of its own dynamics as a group. However, unlike the Tavistock model, the T-group also attended to how individual participants differentiated themselves from one another in terms of particular roles taken within the group structure; for example, some members were quick to emerge as leaders whereas others seemed destined to follow. According to this model these personality differences constituted important data that were to be looked at and talked about by the group. The initial conceptualization and development of the T-group—or "laboratory method," as it is sometimes called—can be attributed to four men: Kurt Lewin and Ronald Lippitt, both social psychologists, and Leland Bradford and Kenneth Benne, both educators. Since Lewin was not only one of the original founders of the model, but also father of the group-dynamics movement in which T-group methodology was initially grounded, it is he to whom primary credit for the model's authorship is usually given. It was Lewin who had first made the study of small-group processes academically respectable and who, through his emphasis on "action research" (Marrow, 1969, p. 158), had encouraged researchers to become actively involved and enmeshed in the very social forces they were bent on studying; in a sense, this approach constituted an application to the social sphere of what, in the area of individual behavior and individual therapy, Sullivan had called "participant-observation" (1953, pp. 13–14). While Lewin's group-dynamics approach had already had an impact on the group-dynamics school of group therapy, this had occurred primarily through the dissemination of his writings and thus had been an indirect influence. The T-group constituted the one model or group interaction with which he was to become personally involved, although he was to die shortly after its initial planning.

Just as the settlement house constituted the applied setting for the development of social group work, and the psychiatric hospital and clinic the background setting for group therapy, business and industry constituted the backdrop for the creation of T-groups. The idea of the model grew out of a conference held in Connecticut in 1946 that had been designed to help business and community leaders implement the Fair Employment Practices Act. At this conference task groups composed of these leaders had been formed for the purpose of discussing the improvement of intergroup relations and the use of groups in developing closer relations among communities. The research arm of the conference was led by Lewin and Lippitt, who held discussions with research personnel in the evening about what could be learned from their observations of the task groups that had met during the day.

Soon it became apparent that the most exciting group discussions were those of the evening research meetings, particularly when participants from the afternoon groups began to attend and to register some dissent, not only as to the accuracy of the observations that had been made of their behavior in the afternoon groups but also as to the interpretations offered to explain this behavior. As these discussions became more heated, Lewin and his co-workers started to see in them the seeds of a related, but more dynamic group (i.e., a "training group," soon to be shortened to "T-group"). Members would have the dual purpose of participating in a group at the same time that they studied their participation and would thus be able to better understand both group process in general and their own individual styles of relating to groups. Such a group would bring into simultaneous operation the processes of participation and observation that the Connecticut conference had separated into two distinct phases, the afternoon group for participation, and the evening group for observation. The sole task of the group would be to understand and to learn from the data of its own behavior. No other agenda would be placed before it, and it would be up to the group to decide how best to proceed with its not too well-defined task. The group leader, or "trainer," would not fulfill the group's probable expectations of how a leader should behave and would instead, in a more indirect and Socratic fashion, ask the kinds of questions and make the kinds of comments that would help the group *learn how to learn* from its experience. Because the group would thus be placed in as pure a culture as possible, the covert group dynamics normally obscured by the pressures, agenda, and structures of ongoing business and bureaucratic groups would be thrown into bolder relief. As a result the participant would hopefully return to his back-home organization with an increased understanding of the processes that can impede a group's performance of its task, and more specifically of how he himself often unwittingly contributes to these impediments. In this sense the changing of systems was as much a goal of the model as was the changing of individuals, although the latter had to be an essential focus if the former was to be achieved. And so the T-group was born.

Although the path from the T-group to the encounter group was not a straightforward one, there can be little doubt that the T-group constitutes its most direct precursor, and many of the men who later became strongly involved in encounter, like William Schutz, initially had been trained at the National Training Laboratory (NTL), the official organization of T-group theorists and trainers. The first significant step taken by NTL toward an encounter emphasis was the introduction into its curriculum of T-groups having "a personal-interpersonal focus," one that directly contrasted with the "group relations and organizational emphasis" inherent in the original T-group. Equally relevant was the evolution of the NTL "Microlab" (Schutz & Seashore, 1972, pp. 191–193), in which a series of nonverbal exercises is employed to create intense interpersonal interactions in a much briefer period of time than is demanded by the less structured conditions of the T-group. Given the temper of the 1960s, which increasingly stressed the importance of openness, it was probably inevitable that the T-group experience would eventually be used as a means of self-discovery and self-expression going beyond a consideration of one's day-to-day functioning in his or her work organization, to the more general question of what kind of work one most wanted to do, or—on the assumption that one possessed adequate financial resources—the question of whether one wanted to work at all! No wonder, then, that by the late 1960s industry had begun to find that for every executive returning from sensitivity-training (now with a clearly encounter focus) as a more competent functionary, there was one who had decided to leave the company (Calame, 1969).

Two particular strains within the culture-at-large helped to hasten the shift within growth and development groups to an encounter focus: an increasing interest in humanistic psychology (which rejected the deterministic thrust of both psychoanalysis and behaviorism, emphasizing instead the person's freedom to choose) and the evolution of the "counterculture" (Roszak, 1969; Reich, 1970), which stressed personal openness and challenged the validity of rational-bureaucratic values, championing instead the expansion of consciousness through a variety of means, including Yoga, meditation, and drugs. The encounter group (as it evolved under the aegis of Bill Schutz at Esalen Institute) was not, unlike its T-group predecessor, at pains to teach participants about group dynamics or to help them relate their group experience to their outside work situation. Instead, through a variety of specific techniques (including psychodrama and gestalt therapy), they would be encouraged to encounter the "true" feeling self that lay hidden beneath their social and professional facades. Also unlike its T-group predecessor, encounter did not make a careful distinction between its purposes and those of therapy groups; therefore, it cannot be divorced from earlier therapy models. Indeed, we view encounter as a logical extension of the various innovations in group therapeutic technique that had preceded it. Once the leader became freer to express himself (existential-experiential), once participants could dramatize their problems, rather than merely narrate them (psychodrama), once group therapy methods were defined as applicable to normal people (gestalt), and once a humanistically oriented counterculture began to question all traditional organizational structures, the freewheeling and relatively loose encounter format was a probably inevitable result.

The theme-centered interactional (TCI) method, the next model to be presented, also shows the influence of several of its predecessors. It was founded by Ruth Cohn, a psychoanalyst and group therapist who wanted to extend the effectiveness of psychotherapeutic methods with individuals to the social malaise of the larger community or culture. Starting with a "countertransference workshop" designed for the group supervision of psychotherapists (Cohn, 1969), she began to develop a model that could apply to many different types of groups where members convened for a common purpose or task. The model's psychotherapeutic heritage was reflected in its constant emphasis on the validity of feelings and on the importance of each participant's stating, whenever possible, his immediate experience. On the other hand, it made a clear-cut distinction between a group designed for therapy and one designed for theme-focused interaction; one of the ways it did this was to formulate specific leadership techniques for bringing back to the theme those participants who were veering off into overly personalized discussion. Since many different kinds of groups, including both committees and classrooms, deal with a common theme or agenda (whether explicitly stated or not), the TCI method could be used for a limitless variety of themes, including "Freedom and Control in the Psychotherapy Relationship" (for therapists), "Live Learning vs. Dead Learning" (for teachers), "Overcoming the Generation Gap" (for parents and teenagers), and "Freeing Creativity" (for writers).

As the theme-centered model began to be introduced by Cohn into Western Europe, where it gained a prominence greater than in the United States, it became clear that several characteristics rendered it antithetical to both the method and spirit of the encounter group. These included an emphasis on the need for occasional discussion in the group of concepts and ideas (as well as of feelings), adapting the group format to the theme-related and outside needs that had brought the group into existence in the first place, and the leader's obligation to protect a member from a deeper emotional experience than the latter had implicitly contracted for. TCI's concern with the group's common goals and expectations bore a strong resemblance to the first model we described, the social work group. Other characteristics shared by both the TCI and social work models are a concern with the larger community context in which a group is embedded and an emphasis on carefully planning each group session beforehand.

The final model that we consider, the self-help group, is clearly a psychotherapy group, yet it is one that has no therapist present. This may initially seem paradoxical, but when one reviews the history of group therapy in detail the eventual emergence of a therapy group without a therapist appears more and more predictable. For example, psychoanalytic groups sometimes have an alternate session where members meet without the group psychoanalyst present, and at its height the encounter movement encouraged the creation of grass-roots groups throughout the nation that would be led by community participants themselves. In a similar vein, Cohn (Cohn & Malamud, 1969) sees TCI's strongest feature to be its adaptability to community settings in which people who share common concerns meet in groups led by the members themselves (with leadership perhaps rotating from one member to the next at successive meetings). Each of these three innovations presaged the eventual emergence of a group model where formal professional leadership would be viewed as at best superfluous, and as at worst antithetical to the group's optimal level of cohesion or vitality.

As we will point out in our concluding chapter, the self-help group furnishes an important connecting link to current trends in group therapy, for (like the TCI group, and other recent groups) it embodies a significant return to emphases that were inherent in the social work model. For instance, if we take Alcholics Anonymous as prototypical of other self-help groups, we find that there is a concern with the common needs of the membership (in this in-